Delicious Christmas

Recipes

A Complete Cookbook Inspired by "A Christmas Carol"!

By: Ronny Emerson

Copyright Notes

Table of Contents

Introduction 6

1 – Heart-Healthy Salad 8

2 – Tarragon Chicken 10

3 – Tasty Egg Salad Sandwiches 12

4 – Oyster Mac 'n' Cheese 15

5 – Blueberry/Banana Smoothie 18

6 – Easy Chocolate Pudding 20

7 – Day-Before-Payday Slow-Cooked Cranberry Chicken 22

8 – Fruitalicious Cranberry Punch 24

9 – Perfect Roast Turkey 26

10 – Perfect Stuffing for Perfect Roast Turkey 29

11 – Savory Mashed Potato Bake 31

12 – Carrot/Turnip Mash 33

13 – Hearty Turkey Soup 35

14 – Winter Beef Stew 39

15 – Velvety Smooth Turkey Gravy 42

16 – Negus 44

17 – Plum Pudding with Spicy Sauce 46

18 – No-Snow Snow Cones 49

19 – Spicy Applesauce 51

20 – Oatmeal Plus 53

21 – Double Cheese Broccoli Casserole 55

22 – Cheesy Jalapeno Pitas 58

23 – Curried Roasted Chestnuts 60

24 – Ghost Pepper Hot Sauce 62

25 – Cheesy Shrimp Toasts 64

26 – Smoked Salmon Breakfast Bagel with Broccoli Leaves 66

27 – Primo Pasta in Red Sauce 68

28 – Wedge Salad with a Difference 70

29 – Devilishly Good Angel Food Cake 72

30 – Day After Christmas Cranberry Sauce Muffins 74

Conclusion 77

Author's Afterthoughts... 78

About the Author 79

Introduction

What did cooks put on the table during the industrial revolution? Usually, it would be something created from whatever ingredients were available. They didn't have the ability to freeze food over the long term the way we can now, so it would have been whatever was in season or available at the market. In spring and summer, fresh greens would have been used. In late summer, fall, and throughout part of the winter, potatoes, turnips, and carrots would have been available. Families that could afford to stock up would have preserved meat and fish for the winter by canning or salting.

Was this a good diet? Not always. We know now that fresh veggies are an important part of a healthy diet, and we also know to avoid excess sodium. Accordingly, while trying to stay true to the spirit of the time during which "A Christmas Carol" is set, I've taken liberties from time to time – using mostly fresh ingredients and reducing the fat and salt that would have been used to excess in the Victorian era.

Food isn't referenced all that much in "A Christmas Carol," and it's a very short book, so at times you may think that I'm "stretching" a bit to give you a recipe that fits the chronology. Am I doing that? Indisputably, yes! Will you forgive me? When you start making these great recipes, I believe you will.

Now, it's time to put on your chef's hat and start cooking. And before you ask, yes, there will be recipes you can use to create the ultimate Christmas dinner. Maybe you can recruit a family member to read "A Christmas Carol" out loud while you cook, creating a beloved Christmas tradition that you'll want to repeat year after year.

1 – Heart-Healthy Salad

The opening line of "A Christmas Carol" reads, "Marley was dead: to begin with." I could complain about the improper use of the colon, but this is a recipe book, not a grammar manual, and besides, it's Dickens! He gets a pass. We're not told what killed Marley, but given that he was a partner in a prosperous firm, there's a good chance that he died of a heart attack after eating too many rich foods. So, let's start with a heart-healthy salad that's rich in antioxidants.

Makes 4 generous servings

Cooking + prep time: about 10 minutes

Ingredients:

- 4 cups mesclun greens
- ½ cup fresh blueberries
- ¼ cup walnut halves
- 6 fresh strawberries, hulled and sliced

Instructions:

Combine all ingredients in a large bowl, and toss.

If you like, you can add a salad dressing of your choice, but you may find that the flavor from the fruit and walnuts makes this unnecessary.

Top with croutons if desired. Serve.

2 – Tarragon Chicken

Here's another heart-friendly recipe that's very easy to make. You can skin the chicken if you like but it will be much juicier if you leave the skin on, and it won't add that much in the way of fat and calories.

Makes 4 servings

Cooking + prep time: about 30 minutes

Ingredients:

- 4 chicken breasts
- 1 tbsp. dried tarragon
- ½ tbsp. garlic powder

Instructions:

Preheat oven to 400F.

Place chicken breasts in shallow dish.

Sprinkle with tarragon and garlic powder.

Bake for 25 minutes.

Serve with baked potatoes or rice.

3 – Tasty Egg Salad Sandwiches

We are told that Scrooge was Marley's sole executor and in charge of his funeral. Being cheap, Scrooge probably wouldn't have put out much of a spread for Marley's wake. You'd think he could at least come up with a few sandwiches, though. Here's a recipe for egg salad sandwiches with a bit of a flavorful twist. The green onion makes the difference!

Makes about 80 small sandwiches, depending on how many slices are in the loaf of bread

Cooking + prep time: about 45 minutes

Ingredients:

- 1 loaf of sliced bread
- 12 hard-boiled eggs
- 2 green onions (green part only), chopped fine
- ¼ tsp. black pepper
- ¼ tsp. paprika
- Butter or margarine, as needed
- Mayonnaise, as desired
- Parsley sprigs, as desired to garnish

Instructions:

Place eggs in a large saucepan and bring to boil.

Turn off heat and allow eggs to sit in the hot water for 12 minutes.

Place eggs in refrigerator to cool.

While eggs are cooling, butter one side of each slice of bread.

When eggs are cool, place them in a large bowl along with the green onions, pepper, and paprika.

Add enough mayonnaise to moisten the egg mixture.

Check for flavor, and if needed, add more mayonnaise.

Spread the egg mixture evenly over buttered bread slices and top with another slice of buttered bread.

Cut diagonally twice, to create 4 triangles.

Serve on a platter, garnished with parsley sprigs.

4 – Oyster Mac 'n' Cheese

Dickens describes Scrooge as "solitary as an oyster." I realize that this is utterly shameless, but I'm going to use that description as an excuse to offer this flavorful oyster recipe. You don't even have to worry about finding fresh oysters – this recipe calls for canned!

Makes 4 servings

Cooking + prep time: 30 minutes

Ingredients:

- 1 ½ cups macaroni or other small pasta
- 1 tbsp. vegetable oil
- ½ cup chopped green pepper
- ¼ cup chopped green onion
- 1 can cheddar cheese soup
- 1 10-oz. can oysters, drained and cut in 2 pieces
- 2 cups cheddar, shredded
- 1 tbsp. Dijon mustard
- Salt to taste (about ½ tsp.)

Instructions:

Preheat oven to 350F

Cook pasta according to package directions.

Heat the oil in a large fry pan.

Add green onion and green pepper and cook until tender.

Stir in the cheddar cheese soup, mustard, and salt.

Add the pasta and oysters.

Stir until blended.

Place half the mixture in a greased casserole dish and top with half of the shredded cheddar.

Add the rest of the pasta/oyster mix and top with the rest of the cheddar.

Bake, covered, for 15 minutes.

Uncover and continue to bake for about 20 minutes, or until bubbly on top.

Serve with green vegetables and crusty bread.

5 – Blueberry/Banana Smoothie

Scrooge's nephew visits him and accuses him of being "morose." Perhaps Scrooge is suffering from clinical depression. Vitamin D is known to help alleviate depression, and this smoothie is just full of D-rich blueberries! Bananas also help to boost Vitamin D, so it's a double threat against depression.

Makes 1 serving

Cooking + prep time: less than 5 minutes

Ingredients:

- 1 cup skim milk
- ½ cup blueberries
- ½ banana
- 1 tbsp. honey
- 1 tsp. vanilla extract

Instructions:

Place all ingredients in a blender jar.

Blend at low speed until smooth.

Garnish with a slice of strawberry if desired, and serve.

6 – Easy Chocolate Pudding

Scrooge tells his nephew that anyone who goes around saying "Merry Christmas" should be "boiled in his own pudding." Wow! That's nasty! But if you have to be boiled in the pudding, you could do a lot worse than this delectable dessert for two.

Makes 2 servings

Cooking + prep time: 15 minutes, not counting cooling

Ingredients:

- 6 tbsp. sugar
- ¼ cup cocoa
- 2 tbsp. cornstarch
- 1 ½ cups milk
- ½ tsp. vanilla extract

Instructions:

In a heavy saucepan, combine the sugar, cocoa, and cornstarch.

Add the milk gradually, and heat until just boiling.

Continue to cook until thickened (about 2 minutes).

Remove from heat.

Stir in the vanilla.

Transfer to serving dishes and place in refrigerator until thoroughly chilled.

Top with whipped cream if desired, and serve.

7 – Day-Before-Payday Slow-Cooked Cranberry Chicken

Scrooge is visited by a pair of philanthropists seeking monetary donations in order to provide "meat and drink" for the poor during the festive season. Scrooge, of course, refuses. Given that there were so many people living in abject poverty at the time, even if Scrooge had been generously disposed, it likely wouldn't have made much of a difference. If you want to stretch your food budget a bit, this flavorful recipe costs very little to make.

Makes 4-8 servings

Cooking + prep time: 4-8 hours

Ingredients:

- 8 skinless chicken thighs
- 1 10-oz. can whole berry cranberry sauce
- 1 cup barbecue sauce

Instructions:

Place chicken thighs in slow cooker.

In a large bowl, mix together the cranberry sauce and barbecue sauce

Pour over chicken thighs

Cook on high for 4 hours or on low for 8 hours

Serve over rice.

8 – Fruitalicious Cranberry Punch

Well, I did say meat and *drink,* didn't I? Christmas and cranberries seem inextricably bound, so they're a perfect fit for this festive punch. If you want a non-alcoholic offering, this is equally good if you omit the spirits.

Makes 24 servings

Cooking + prep time: about 10 minutes, not counting time to freeze the ice block

Ingredients:

- 1 quart cranberry cocktail
- 1 quart sparkling lemonade
- 1 quart vodka or white rum
- 2 cups pineapple juice
- 1 lemon, sliced
- 1 cup whole cranberries
- 1 ice mold

Instructions:

The night before, make the ice mold. Fill a gelatin mold, Bundt cake pan, or even a bowl, with water and place in freezer.

About an hour before you're ready to serve the punch, pour the liquids into a large punch bowl.

Add the lemon slices and whole cranberries for garnish.

Gently slide in the ice mold.

Provide punch cups, and let your guests serve themselves.

9 – Perfect Roast Turkey

The poor freeze in the streets, while the Lord Mayor orders his 50 cooks to prepare for Christmas as befitting his station. With 50 cooks, one would imagine that he's gearing up for quite the feast and will require a lot of turkeys. You, however, can feel free to cook just one! This recipe improves on pre-basted turkeys because you'll be using all-natural butter instead of the broth, sugar, and salt used in the pre-basted birds. It requires a bit of work (and one special item – a syringe) but the results are well worth it.

Servings depend on the size of the bird – allow 4-6 ounces of meat per person

Cooking + prep time: 13-15 minutes per pound to cook and 20 minutes to prepare (cooking time does not include preparing stuffing)

Ingredients:

- 1 turkey, 15-20 pounds
- 1/3 cup melted butter
- Salt, as desired
- Pepper, as desired
- 1 sprig fresh rosemary and 1 sprig fresh sage (if not using stuffing)

Instructions:

Purchase a syringe with needle from your local drugstore or farm supply store.

Preheat oven to 350F.

If your turkey comes with giblets, liver, neck, and heart, remove them from the body cavity and place in pan along with turkey – you can use them to make gravy after the turkey is cooked.

Using a paper towel, wipe out the inside of the turkey's body cavity.

Stuff if desired (see recipe 10).

If not stuffing, place the rosemary and sage in the body cavity.

Place the turkey in a roasting pan, breast side up.

Attach the needle to the syringe, and draw the melted butter up into the syringe.

Holding the needle at a 45-degree angle, gently slide it under the skin of the bird and inject a small amount of melted butter under the skin at approximately 1-1/2 inches intervals. Continue until the butter is evenly distributed and used up.

Rub the skin of the turkey with salt and pepper.

Roast, uncovered, 13 minutes per pound for unstuffed turkey and 15 minutes per pound for stuffed. The turkey is done when the thigh joint moves easily away from the body.

Remove from oven and let stand for about half the cooking time – this allows the juices to distribute evenly throughout the bird.

10 – Perfect Stuffing for Perfect Roast Turkey

This is a simple bread stuffing that you can't ruin because there's so much flexibility in the ingredients. For that reason, you'll find the ingredients in approximate measures. You can adjust the level of herbs and spices to suit your personal taste or that of your family.

Makes enough stuffing for 15-20 pounds turkey, with some left over

Cooking + prep time: 30 minutes

Ingredients:

- 1 loaf white bread (if it's stale, that's fine)
- 2 tbsp. summer savory
- ¼ tsp. pepper
- ¼ tsp. salt

Instructions:

Tear the bread into pieces, about ½ inch each.

Place bread in bowl and toss with summer savory, pepper, and salt.

Place stuffing mix in turkey body and neck cavity.

If you have leftover stuffing mix and want to create more stuffing, boil a potato and mash it. Add to leftover stuffing mix, blend well, and place in greased dish. Cook in oven along with turkey. It will be done in about half an hour.

11 – Savory Mashed Potato Bake

Potatoes were a staple for poor people at the time of the industrial revolution. If you're cooking potatoes for extra stuffing, do a few more for this delicious baked dish.

Makes 4 servings

Cooking + prep time: about an hour

Ingredients:

- 4 cups mashed potatoes
- 1 cup grated old cheddar
- ¼ cup grated onion
- Butter, as needed

Instructions:

Preheat oven to 350F.

Using a pastry blender, mix together the mashed potatoes and cheese.

Add onion and mix well.

Grease a 2-quart casserole dish using the butter.

Place potato mixture in greased casserole dish.

Dot with butter.

Bake for 30-45 minutes, or until top is browned.

12 – Carrot/Turnip Mash

Poor people at the time of the industrial revolution would have relied heavily on root vegetables. This is a root vegetable mix that goes well with the above potato dish. It's easy to make and very delicious.

Makes 4 servings

Cooking + prep time: 45 minutes

Ingredients:

- 1 pound carrots
- 1 pound turnips
- ¼ cup butter

Instructions:

Cook carrots and turnips until soft.

Drain, add butter, and mash.

13 – Hearty Turkey Soup

Being parsimonious (to put it mildly), I doubt if Scrooge would ever have allowed anything to go to waste. He would certainly have approved of this wonderfully filling soup that you can make from inexpensive vegetables and your post-Christmas turkey carcass that would otherwise be thrown out. You'd be surprised at how much meat you can get off a boiled carcass, even if you think there's not much left!

Makes about 12 servings, depending on the size of your stock pot

Cooking + prep time: About 1 day + 5 hours (sounds scarier than it is, so please keep reading)

Ingredients:

- 1 turkey carcass (see note 1)
- 1 onion, skin left on
- 1 whole carrot
- 1 bay leaf
- 1 tsp. soy sauce
- Water to cover (see note 2)
- 5 carrots, peeled and cut in ¼-inch pieces
- 1 small rutabaga, peeled and cut in ¼-inch pieces
- 2 large potatoes, peeled and cut in ¼-inch pieces
- 1 onion, peeled and diced
- 1 tbsp. summer savory
- ¼ tsp. dried sage
- ¼ tsp. dried rosemary
- Salt and pepper to taste
- 1 cup frozen green beans

Instructions:

Prepare the turkey carcass by cracking the bones as much as possible.

Place the turkey carcass in a large stockpot. Add the un-skinned onion, whole carrot, bay leaf, and soy sauce.

Cover with water and bring to a boil.

Reduce heat and simmer for 3-4 hours.

Remove turkey carcass, place it in a large bowl, and discard the onion, carrot, and bay leaf.

Strain the turkey stock through a large colander into another large pot and place in refrigerator, covered, to cool.

Allow the turkey carcass to cool and then pick off as much meat as possible. Place in a container in the refrigerator for use the following day.

The next day, any fat remaining in the stock will have solidified and risen to the top. Using a slotted spoon, remove and discard the fat.

Return the stock to your stock pot.

Add the diced carrots and rutabaga, and bring to a boil.

Reduce heat to simmer, and cook until the vegetables are somewhat tender but not quite cooked.

Add the diced potatoes, onion, and turkey, and cook until all vegetables are fork-tender.

Add the herbs and spices in the last half hour of cooking.

Check for seasoning, and add salt if needed.

Add green beans and continue simmering for 10 minutes.

Serve with crusty bread.

Note 1: If you are using a turkey that has been roasted with bread stuffing, scrape as much of the stuffing as possible out of the cavity. The more bread is left, the cloudier the stock will be. This won't affect the flavor, but a clear stock is more pleasing to the eye.

Note 2: Depending on the size of your turkey carcass and the amount of meat remaining on it, you may find that the stock is not overly robust. If that's the case, you can add chicken bouillon cubes, one at a time, until you get the flavor you want.

14 – Winter Beef Stew

The Lord Mayor must have been a hard-hearted soul, since we're told that at the height of the holiday season, he fined a tailor five shillings for public drunkenness. That would have been a great hardship for a tradesperson at the time, but even so, the tailor managed to retain enough money to send his wife out to buy beef for their dinner. With the addition of winter vegetables, perhaps she created something like this delicious beef stew.

Makes about 8 servings

Cooking + prep time: about 3 1/2 hours

Ingredients:

- ¼ cup extra virgin olive oil
- ¼ slice of white bread
- 2 lbs. stewing beef (use the fatty kind – it makes for better flavor)
- 1 large onion, cut in chunks
- 6 carrots, cut in chunks
- 1 small rutabaga, cut in chunks
- 3 large potatoes, peeled and cut in chunks
- 1 bay leaf
- Water to cover
- ¼ tsp. ground sage
- Salt and pepper to taste
- 1 tbsp. corn starch mixed in ½ cup of water

Instructions:

In a large pot, heat the olive oil.

When it looks like the oil is hot enough (but before it begins to smoke), add the piece of bread. When it's lightly browned, that means the oil is hot enough.

Remove the bread and add the beef and onion, stirring occasionally until the beef is browned on all sides.

Add the carrots, rutabaga, and bay leaf.

If you like, at this point you can also add the potato chunks. However, since potatoes take less time to cook, you will have a better stew if you boil the potatoes separately and add them to the rest of the stew just before serving.

Add water just to cover.

Bring to a boil.

Reduce heat and simmer for 3 hours.

During the last half hour of cooking, add the sage, salt, and pepper.

Bring the stew to a boil and stir in the corn starch mixture.

Stir until thickened, and serve.

15 – Velvety Smooth Turkey Gravy

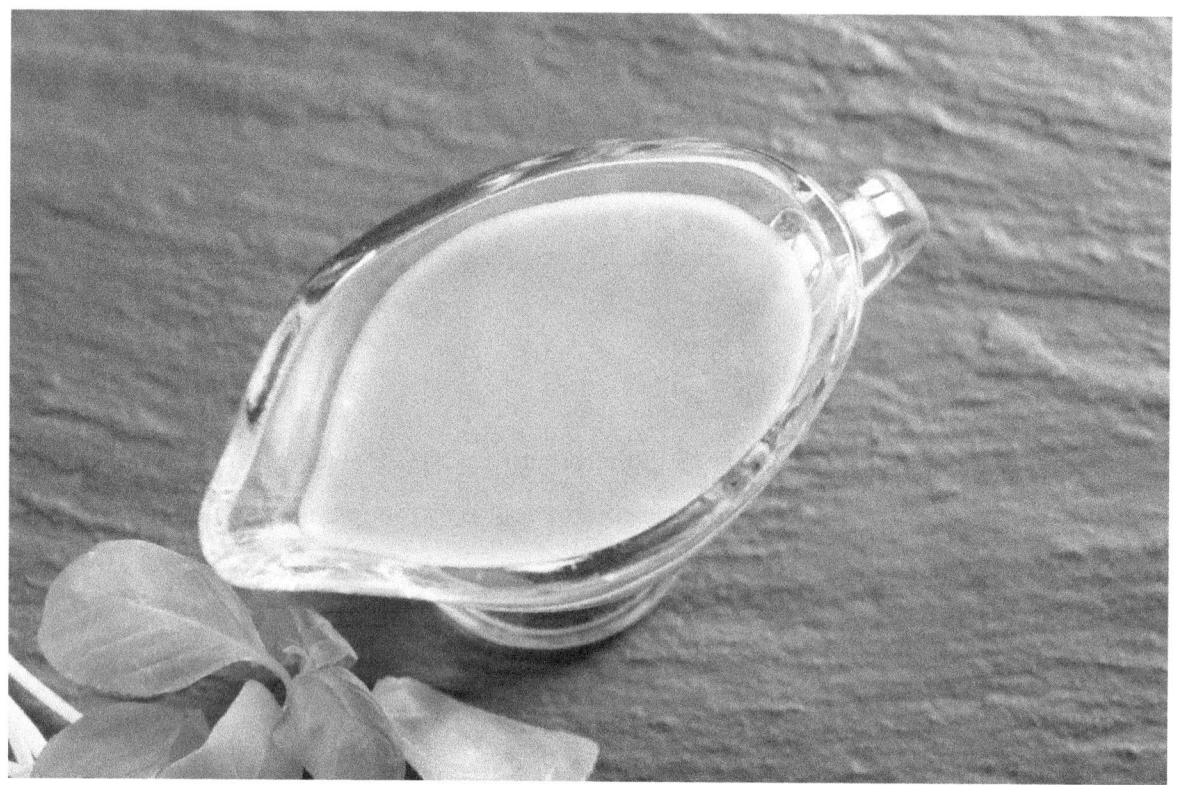

Scrooge takes his long-suffering employee, Bob Cratchit, to task for wanting a half-day off at Christmas. Then he goes home to his lonely rooms, where he encounters the ghost of his erstwhile partner, Jacob Marley. At first, Scrooge refuses to believe that he's actually seeing a ghost, blaming the apparition on bad digestion – he must have eaten something that was bad for him! "There's more of gravy than of grave about you," he tells the ghost. Time for a gravy recipe?

Makes about 1 ½ pints of gravy

Cooking + prep time: 10 minutes

Ingredients:

- Turkey drippings, as needed
- 1 cup water
- 1 cup milk
- ¼ tsp. dried sage
- ½ tbsp. corn starch, mixed in ¼ cup of water
- Salt and pepper to taste

Instructions:

Remove your turkey from the roasting pan and scrape the drippings into a medium-size pot.

Add water and milk.

Add sage.

Bring to a boil.

Add corn starch mixture and cook at a boil until thickened.

Check for seasoning, and add salt and pepper if needed.

16 – Negus

Marley tells Scrooge that he is there to help him see the error of his ways and become a better person. He states that Scrooge will be visited by three spirits that will help him. The first is the Ghost of Christmas Past, who takes Scrooge on a journey through his previous Christmases, both sad and happy. One stop is a look back at Fezziwig's ball, where Scrooge's former employer once hosted a marvelous party with dancing, games, and wondrous food and drink, including negus, a mulled port offering.

Makes 16 4-oz. servings

Cooking + prep time: 30 minutes

Ingredients:

- 1 qt. port wine
- 1 tbsp. sugar
- Juice of 1 lemon
- Juice of 1 orange
- Grated rind of 1 lemon
- ¼ tsp. ground cinnamon
- Pinch of ground cloves
- 1 qt. boiling water

Instructions:

In a large pot, heat the port until fine bubbles begin to appear, but do not let it boil.

Add the sugar, juices, lemon rind, and spices.

Remove from heat and let stand for 15 minutes.

Pour in the boiling water and serve immediately.

If you like, you can put a slice of lemon or orange in each cup for garnish.

17 – Plum Pudding with Spicy Sauce

Scrooge meets the next spirit when he sees a ghostly light coming from what appears to be an adjacent room. He opens the door, and sees that it is actually his own room, but greatly transformed – festooned with holly, mistletoe, and ivy, and heaped high with all manner of meat, poultry, cake, fruit, plum pudding, and more. Plum pudding has long been a staple of Christmas feasts, but did you know that it doesn't contain plums?

Makes 2 puddings

Cooking + prep time: 1-3 weeks (about 6 hours for the actual prep; the rest is refrigeration time)

Ingredients:

- 1 cup softened butter
- 1 cup white sugar
- 2 beaten eggs
- 1 cup milk
- 2/3 cup molasses
- 3 tbsp. baking powder
- 1 tsp. baking soda
- 1/4 tsp. salt
- 3 1/2 cups plus 2 tbsp. flour
- 1 1/2 cups chopped golden raisins
- 1 cup chopped dates
- 1/2 cups walnut pieces
- 1 1/2 cups chopped apples
- 3 tbsp. chopped candied citron
- 1 tsp. ground cinnamon
- 1/4 tsp. ground nutmeg
- Boiling water, as needed

Sauce:

- 2/3 cup white sugar
- 1 1/2 tsp. cornstarch
- 1/8 tsp. salt
- 1 cup boiling water
- 1 tbsp. butter
- 1/2 teaspoon ground nutmeg

Instructions:

Grease 2 2-quart pudding molds or deep oven-proof dishes.

In a large bowl, combine all the ingredients except for the boiling water.

When the batter is smooth and even, fill each baking dish about halfway.

Cover the dishes with lids or 2 thicknesses of aluminum foil and place on a rack in a large roaster or pot.

Fill with boiling water about 2/3 of the way up the dishes.

Cover the roaster or pot and boil gently for about 4 ½ hours or until a knife comes out clean when inserted into the center of the pudding. Add more boiling water if the level drops below 2/3.

Allow the puddings to cool at room temperature.

When thoroughly cooled, wrap in plastic film and place in sealed freezer bags, making sure to squeeze out all the air.

Refrigerate for at least a week – the puddings will keep refrigerated for up to 3 weeks.

Reheat before serving. You can do this in a boiling water bath, but simply microwaving them is easier and less time-consuming.

To make the sauce, which you will drizzle over the pudding before serving, simply combine all ingredients in a saucepan and boil for about 3 minutes or until the mixture is smooth.

18 – No-Snow Snow Cones

Scrooge feels that he has learned something about the true meaning of Christmas from the previous spirit and bids the Ghost of Christmas present to do with him whatever he feels is necessary. They head out on their journey, and one of the first things Scrooge observes is happy villagers shoveling away snow and throwing snowballs at one another. With an abundance of snow, perhaps they also made snow cones! Of course, not everyone lives in a winter wonderland, so this super-easy recipe for snow cones substitutes crushed ice.

Makes 8 Servings

Cooking + prep time: about 10 minutes

Ingredients:

- ¾ cup sugar-sweetened drink mix (you can use Kool-Aid, Tang, or any generic drink mix)
- ½ cup cold water
- 8 cups crushed ice (you can make it by whirling ice cubes in a blender or food processor)

Instructions:

Place drink mix and water in a small bowl and stir until dissolved.

Divide the crushed ice equally amongst 8 serving cups.

Drizzle 1 tbsp. of the drink mixture over each serving.

Insert a spoon or straw in each cup and serve.

19 – Spicy Applesauce

Scrooge and the spirit look in on Bob Cratchit's home, where in spite of the pittance Scrooge pays him, Bob has managed to provide a good Christmas dinner consisting of roast goose, vegetables, and Mrs. Cratchit's own homemade applesauce. Spices were expensive back then, but I'd like to think that she'd have had a bit of cinnamon to flavor this simple sauce.

Makes 4 servings

Cooking + prep time: 15 minutes

Ingredients:

- 4 Granny Smith apples
- 3/4 cups water
- 1/4 cup granulated sugar
- 1/2 tsp. ground cinnamon

Instructions:

Peel, core, and slice the apples.

Place in a small saucepan along with the water, sugar, and cinnamon.

Boil until the apples are tender, almost mushy.

Mash and serve hot, or chill to use later.

20 – Oatmeal Plus

Bob wants to raise a toast to Scrooge for providing him with the livelihood needed to create their Christmas feast. Mrs. Cratchit is having none of it, saying that Scrooge is an "odious, stingy, hard, unfeeling man." She also snipes that she's looking forward to a long rest in bed the following day after drinking to Scrooge's health. Do you suppose she's going to need a hangover cure? If so, she could do worse than this oatmeal dish, which is easy on the stomach and also contains B vitamins and other nutrients that repair the body after a night of excess.

Makes 6 servings

Cooking + prep time: 15 minutes

Ingredients:

- 2 ¼ cups water
- 1 cup quick oats
- 1 tbsp. wheat bran
- 1 tbsp. wheat germ
- 1 tbsp. flax seed
- ¼ tsp. dried cinnamon

Instructions:

Place all the ingredients in a saucepan. Bring to boil.

Cook at high for 5 minutes.

Remove from the heat. Allow to stand for 5 minutes.

Serve with milk or cream, along with honey or brown sugar to taste.

21 – Double Cheese Broccoli Casserole

Although the Cratchits are enjoying Christmas, they don't know what the future holds. Their youngest child, Tiny Tim, is not well. We're not told exactly what ails him, but he walks with a crutch, which might suggest a disorder of the leg bones - not uncommon in industrial-era children who often didn't get anywhere near enough calcium and vitamins in their diet. This broccoli casserole is ideal for promoting healthy bone growth.

Makes 4 large servings

Cooking + prep time: 1 hour

Ingredients:

- 4 cups water
- 4 cups broccoli florets
- 1 cup diced onion
- 4 garlic cloves, minced
- 2 tbsp. butter
- 1 x 10 & 1/2-oz. can cream of mushroom soup
- 2 cups shredded old cheddar
- 6 ounces cream cheese
- 1/2 cup chicken broth
- 2 tsp. Worcestershire sauce
- 3/4 tsp. black pepper
- 1/2 tsp. salt
- 2 slices whole wheat bread, buttered

Instructions:

Preheat oven to 350F.

In a large saucepan, bring water to boil.

Add broccoli florets and return to boil.

Reduce heat and simmer for about 5 minutes or until broccoli is tender.

Drain and set aside.

In a heavy pan, fry the onion and garlic in butter until just tender.

Add to saucepan.

Add soup, cheeses, chicken broth, Worcestershire sauce, pepper, and salt.

Cook over low heat until cheeses melt, and all ingredients are well-blended.

Transfer the mixture to a large, greased baking dish.

Whirl the buttered bread in a blender or food processor to create fine crumbs and use to top the casserole.

Cook in oven for 30 minutes.

Allow to stand for 10 minutes and serve.

22 – Cheesy Jalapeno Pitas

Scrooge's social conscience is beginning to emerge, and he worries that Tiny Tim might die. He implores the spirit to tell him that this will not be the case. The spirit isn't cutting Scrooge any slack and offers a very Scrooge-like take on the situation. If Tim does die, the spirit opines, it will "decrease the surplus population." I guess a sharp comment like that warrants a sharp recipe, like this spicy lunch dish!

Makes 4 servings

Cooking + prep time: 15 minutes

Ingredients:

- 4 x 8-inch pita breads
- 1 lb. lean ground beef
- 1 small onion, diced
- 1 jalapeno pepper, chopped fine
- ¼ cup extra virgin olive oil
- 1 cup hot salsa
- 1 cup shredded Monterey Jack cheese
- Sour cream, as desired, for dipping

Instructions:

In heavy pan, cook the ground beef, onion, and jalapeno pepper in olive oil until meat is browned.

Add salsa and cheese and continue cooking until cheese is melted.

Stuff pitas with the meat mixture.

Microwave for about 15 seconds – just until the pita bread is warmed.

Serve with sour cream, as desired.

23 – Curried Roasted Chestnuts

Scrooge and the ghost visit the home of Scrooge's nephew, Fred, where Christmas is being celebrated joyously. Scrooge is somewhat chagrined to discover that they are making fun of him because every year they invite him to Christmas dinner, and every year he refuses the invitation. Scrooge, at this point, would have accepted their invitation, but the ghost whisks him away. You'd think they could at least have stopped to enjoy some roasted chestnuts!

Makes 4 Servings

Cooking + prep time: 10 minutes

Ingredients:

- 1 pound chestnuts
- 1 tbsp. curry powder
- 1 tsp. turmeric
- ½ tsp. kosher salt

Instructions:

Preheat oven to 425F.

Place chestnuts on a cutting board.

Using a serrated knife, cut down the long side of each chestnut.

Place chestnuts in a large saucepan and cover with cold water.

Bring to a boil and then immediately remove the chestnuts and place in large bowl.

Add the curry powder, turmeric, and salt, and toss until coated.

Place chestnuts, cut side up, in a baking pan, separating them by about half an inch.

Bake for 20 minutes.

Remove chestnuts from pan and wrap in clean towel.

Let stand for 15 minutes and serve.

24 – Ghost Pepper Hot Sauce

The next spirit is the Ghost of Christmas Yet to Come, and the one that Scrooge fears most. With good reason, as it turns out. The spirit shows him a man who died alone and un-mourned, and a child, also dead, but very much mourned. Scrooge begs to know who the man was and learns that it was none other than himself. The child was Tiny Tim. Well, we know where Scrooge is going to end up after he dies, if he doesn't change his ways, and it will be pretty hot. Kind of like this ghost pepper sauce.

Makes 20 servings

Cooking + prep time: 30 minutes

Ingredients:

- 1 tbsp. olive oil
- 6 ghost peppers, diced
- 2 tomatoes, chopped
- 1 small onion, diced
- 1/2 cup water
- 2 tbsp. red wine vinegar
- 1 tsp. salt

Instructions:

Dice the peppers – make sure to wear gloves, since ghost peppers are the hottest you can buy, and they'll burn your hands if they're not protected.

Chop the tomatoes.

Dice the onions.

Place the peppers, tomatoes, and onion in a small sauce pot and add the water, vinegar, and salt.

Bring to a boil.

Reduce heat and simmer for 20 minutes.

Transfer the mixture to a blender or food processor and blend until smooth.

Place in jars or containers and refrigerate until ready to use – this mixture will keep for several weeks.

25 – Cheesy Shrimp Toasts

Scrooge vows to be a better man and keep Christmas in his heart. He doesn't want to die un-mourned, and, more important, he doesn't want Tiny Tim to die. He begins by sending a huge turkey to Bob Cratchit's family, and then visiting his nephew, Fred, in order to have Christmas dinner with Fred and his family. Perhaps they would have begun with this delicious appetizer. It's easy to make and very tasty.

Makes 24 servings

Cooking + prep time: 30 minutes

Ingredients:

- 6 slices toasted sourdough bread, cut in quarters
- 1 x 6-oz. can salad shrimp, mashed
- ¼ cup cream cheese
- 1/8 cup mayonnaise
- 1 tsp. dried parsley
- ¼ tsp. pepper
- ¼ tsp. salt

Instructions:

Toast and quarter the sourdough bread.

Mix together the remaining ingredients.

Spread on top of the toasted sourdough quarters and serve.

If you like, you can garnish with a parsley spring.

26 – Smoked Salmon Breakfast Bagel with Broccoli Leaves

Scrooge goes to his office, hoping to meet Bob Cratchit. He does, because Bob still doesn't know that Scrooge has reformed. Scrooge berates Bob for showing up to work and offers him a raise! I figure the only way Scrooge could have done better would be if he'd brought breakfast along. This is a delicious twist on the typical breakfast sandwich, making use of now-trendy broccoli leaves.

Makes 1 serving

Cooking + prep time: 15 minutes

Ingredients:

- 1 bagel, split and toasted
- 1/8 cup garlic cream cheese
- ½ cup fresh broccoli leaves
- 2 slices smoked salmon
- Salt & pepper to taste

Instructions:

Spread half of the bagel with cream cheese and top with smoked salmon and broccoli leaves.

Add salt & pepper as desired.

Microwave just long enough to melt the cheese, wilt the broccoli, and warm smoked salmon – about 30 seconds on high.

27 – Primo Pasta in Red Sauce

Tiny Tim lives, and Scrooge becomes something like a second father to him. He also becomes more than an employer to Bob – something very like a friend. Mrs. Cratchit, who had harsh things to say about him, presumably came around and might even have invited him over for a family dinner. In this day and age, you might serve family and close friends something like this pasta dish.

Makes 6 servings

Cooking + prep time: about 1 hour

Ingredients:

- 8 cups cooked noodles or macaroni
- ¼ cup extra virgin olive oil
- 1 lb. ground beef
- 1 small onion, diced
- 1 8-oz. can or 14-oz. jar store-bought spaghetti sauce
- 1 28-oz. can stewed tomatoes, drained and crushed (you can use your hands to crush the tomatoes)
- 1 tsp. dried basil
- 1 tsp. dried rosemary
- 1 tbsp. dried parsley
- ¼ tsp. ground red pepper
- ¼ tsp. salt
- Parmesan cheese and dried chiles, as desired

Instructions:

In large saucepan, brown the meat and onion in olive oil.

Add the spaghetti sauce, crushed tomatoes, basil, rosemary, parsley, red pepper, and salt.

Heat to just before boiling.

Reduce heat and simmer for half an hour.

Serve over hot cooked pasta.

Top with grated parmesan cheese and dried chiles if desired.

28 – Wedge Salad with a Difference

Today, many people choose to follow the main course with a palate-cleansing salad instead of dessert. In Mrs. Cratchit's day, a wedge salad would likely have consisted of just ¼ of a head of iceberg lettuce and perhaps an oil and vinegar dressing. This version takes it to the next level.

Makes 4 servings

Cooking + prep time: 10 minutes

Ingredients:

- 1 head iceberg lettuce
- 2 ripe peaches, sliced
- 1 cup bottled blue cheese dressing
- ½ cup crumbled blue cheese

Instructions:

Quarter the lettuce head, removing the core.

Place each lettuce quarter on a serving plate.

Surround with sliced peaches, evenly divided.

Add blue cheese dressing, ¼ cup for each lettuce quarter.

Top each with 1/8 cup crumbled blue cheese. Serve.

29 – Devilishly Good Angel Food Cake

Is Scrooge truly reformed, or is he just afraid of dying? I think that Dickens wrote this novella well enough that we have to believe that Scrooge's redemption is real. And he's probably not going to end up in hell. Accordingly, here's a great recipe for angel food cake!

Makes about 8 servings

Cooking + prep time: 15 minutes

Ingredients:

- 1 cup flour
- 1 1/2 cups confectioner's sugar
- 12 egg whites, large
- 1 1/4 tsp. cream of tartar
- 1 tsp. salt
- 1 tsp. vanilla
- 1 tsp. almond extract, pure

Instructions:

Do not pre-heat the oven.

Sift flour and sugar together several times.

In a separate bowl, beat egg whites until foamy.

Add cream of tartar and salt.

Fold the egg white mixture gently into the dry ingredients

Pour into 10-inch tube pan.

Turn the oven on and set at 325F.

Cook the cake for about an hour, or until golden brown.

Invert the cake onto a rack and let cool in pan.

Remove when completely cooled, and ice or decorate as desired.

30 – Day After Christmas Cranberry Sauce Muffins

I figure that at this point, Scrooge is such a nice guy he's probably even allowing Bob a couple of breaks throughout the workday! Perhaps the two men, who are now friends instead of just employer and employee, can take a bit of time to enjoy a cup of coffee and one of these hearty muffins. They're a great way to use up any cranberry sauce leftover from Christmas dinner!

Makes 18 servings

Cooking + prep time: 45 minutes

Ingredients:

- 1 ½ cups white flour
- 1/2 cup whole wheat flour
- ¼ cup brown sugar
- 3/4 cup white sugar
- 1/2 tsp. salt
- 3 tsp. baking powder
- 1 cup partially skimmed milk
- 1/2 tsp. vanilla
- 1/4 cup sunflower oil
- 1 beaten egg
- 1 cup whole berry cranberry sauce

Instructions:

Preheat oven to 400F.

Line muffin cups with paper liners.

In a large bowl, mix together the dry ingredients.

Make a well in the middle and add the milk, sunflower oil, vanilla, and beaten egg.

Stir until the ingredients are combined, and then stir in the cranberry sauce.

Fill each muffin cup about 3/4 full.

Bake for 20 minutes.

Cool slightly and serve.

Conclusion

This cookbook based on "A Christmas Carol" has shown you…

… an array of recipes that are ideal for the holidays, or for any other time of year. You've also had a look at a very bleak time in history – one in which society was very much divided into "haves" and "have nots." For many of the working class, a sumptuous Christmas dinner (like the one you can create using these recipes) would have been nothing more than a dream.

Do you believe in ghosts? Was Scrooge really visited by spirits or did he simply have a dream generated by his own guilty conscience? I think "A Christmas Carol" is a ghost story in the truest sense of the word. It's made very clear in the beginning that Scrooge is a nasty, nasty man, and I very much doubt that his conscience would have suddenly been awakened on Christmas Eve without a little help.

I re-read "A Christmas Carol" every year during breaks from Christmas cooking, and I'm always moved by the thread of hope that runs consistently throughout the book – the idea that redemption is available to anyone, provided that they open their hearts. I'm also reminded that a good heart is its own reward – in the beginning Bob Cratchit has very little, thanks to Scrooge, and yet he is kindly disposed toward the man.

Are you ready to start cooking? Pick a recipe, assemble the ingredients, and get to work. You might also pour yourself a mug of Negus and, as did Bob Cratchit, offer a toast to Ebenezer Scrooge!

Author's Afterthoughts

The fact that you all have read this book means more than you know. However, I've seen how much feedback has helped me grow in the last few years. Those comments on things that I have unintentionally overlooked make me go back to the drawing board. I would love you to leave some feedback as well. This will be useful in making sure I churn out high-quality books for you all the time. Also, it doesn't hurt that your feedback will help guide those searching for the right book.

Thanks,

Ronny Emerson

About the Author

Ronny Emerson is mostly referred to as magic fingers. He has the unique ability to create the best dishes out of ordinary ingredients. This skilled culinary professional is recognized for his contributions to the creation of exceptional gastronomic delights. After he won his first cooking contest at 9, there was nowhere else to go but up. His father has always been his role model for cooking tasty dishes. It was under his tutelage that he grew to become the professional we know today.

Ronny travels around the world, where he samples different cuisine from diverse cultures. He cherishes the opportunity to enjoy the various flavors from these restaurants. With what he has learned on his travels, Ronny heads home to his base in New York, where he makes his unique recipes with a brilliant blend of these cultures. So far, he has found comfort in working for one of the top restaurants in the city as the executive chef. Ronny also loves to share what he comes up with in the kitchen.